No • Three

Get Your Mind Right

You hold in your hand *Tight* 3, which is a 2008 Shires Press Paperback Edition. You know, Shires Press: 4869 Main Street (P.O. Box 2200), Manchester Center, Vermont 05255. If you have Internet access, you can find more at www.northshire.com/printondemand.php. I'm sure you want to know about the copyright too. OK. © **2008 by Contributors Herein.** If you got your mind right and wish to reproduce any of the work from *Tight* 3, you should contact the person who wrote said work. It's theirs. Be sure to give credit to *Tight* as well; it's ours. But most importantly, now, it's yours. Find us at tightjournal.blogspot.com. The design for this issue was done by The Doctor, based on original concepts by The Mayor and The Sheriff. For those who care about such things, the body text is set in 10/12 point Century Schoolbook. *Tight* is printed using 100% recycled paper. We love baby animals as well. Printed in the United States of America by Northshire Press using an Espresso Book Machine from On Demand Books. The Northshire Bookstore joins only four other locations in the world that currently or will soon have an Espresso Book Machine: Open Content Alliance (San Francisco, California); the University of Alberta campus bookstore (Edmonton, Alberta, Canada); Bibliotheca Alexandrina (Library of Alexandria; Alexandria, Egypt); and the New Orleans Public Library (New Orleans, Louisiana). ISBN 978-1-60571-002-0

TIGHT
← →

TIGHT
← →

David Berman | 1 | Andrew Mister | 2 | Ryan Murphy | 9 |

Lisa Jarnot | 13 | James Meetze | 14 | Gabriel Gudding | 16 |

David Huddle | 21 | Sommer Browning | 23 | Evan Kennedy | 28 |

Arlo Quint | 30 | Daniel Nester | 32 | Sandra Simonds | 39 |

Shanna Compton | 43 | John Koethe | 46 | Cate Peebles | 49 |

Mike Hauser | 52 | Buck Downs | 54 | Aaron Belz | 56 |

Nora Almeida | 60 | Michael Carr | 62 | Mark Horosky | 65 |

Jess Mynes | 68 | Charles Wright | 71 | Katy Henriksen | 73 |

Chris Martin | 77 | Matt Hart | 82 | Jill Alexander Essbaum | 87 |

Robert Kelly | 90 | Kathleen Winter | 97 | Morgan Lucas Schuldt | 99 |

Maurice Manning | 103 | Ed Skoog | 109 | Joseph Massey | 112 |

DAVID BERMAN

↤ ↦

A Note

resolve to send poem to tight.
non-compliance will break the
combination of the hot tears
of shame ducts

best

DCB

ANDREW MISTER

Song Cycle

State what is literally the case
Broken weather into strands
Of smoke and ash and other things
We would rather regret than remake

Other time of night, of not remembering
Where there once was somewhere
My father, lonely communist
His daughter, she died

*

Still drunk in its soothing souvenirs
My hometown, a lonely crawl
Across the American lawn
God bless you, good morning

A decade of Autumns
With nowhere else to go
High because we have to
My hometown, it drowned

Another advertisement
An admission of guilt
As if to say
I am standing here

I will keep standing
Here among the hashers
Like the world, my own bad son
Bent into shape

*

Meant to spill over
From one mouth to another
Honey lemon throat coat
Tired tape machine

Not a song as much as
An album of songs
Brink of the clouds
Sewn to the sky

God send your sons home
By god I mean anyone stronger than me
By strength I mean the ability to cause pain
One less one less one

Give me difference; give me repetition
There are only so many words
Placement doesn't make a difference
Argument in order to speak

*

Who's going to love you the best
A certain sadness
Walking to McDonald's
Beneath the sky's golden arch

The current conflict, the current
Don't touch me—and you don't
The only difference
That same someone

Self-storage
Still sick summer
A noise beneath the noise
Glenn Gould humming

Tape hiss is a language
Wind raked through leaves
Cookie monster libretto
Howl mockery at the cross

*

The freedom of the Frigidaire
Which sea shall swallow me
Night's rental car glow
Momentarily illuminated by street light

Brailled along the alleyways
Andrew Mister (public domain)
A footnote, a fire escape
Poem without end, a lifetime

Live free or don't
The New Loneliness, LLC
A hall monitor's fate
Two or three things I know about her

Awakening or over-sleeping
Afraid of being left alone
Appetite and/or weight loss
Nothing happens until it stops

*

Play me a song, Jonathan Peel
A calm to call my own
How much have you changed
Since you started writing this poem

No longer sleeps alone
Sometimes cries for no reason
May cause drowsiness
All of the above

There is a line to be drawn
The edge of our bodies
A good ex-girlfriend
Is hard to find

Found sound, a requiem
Each day we begin and end
The slow sick sucking part of me
All contracts are binding

*

A season to come out of changed
Awoke in the werewolf song
Copied down certain lines
Erased them, repeat after me

Remember the doomsday cults
Venom, Kreator, Merciful Fate
Every day has a saviour
Calling in sick, getting high in the morning

Burn all my money
To make more money
We all work in dust
Nude descending, Lucifer Rising

Cornell caught sight of
A sea of buildings
And birds between them
To make nothing new

*

We will all eat dirt, sing along
View east from the top of the B&O trestle
Who could ask for more
Lying in bed listening to

The soft flutter of your veins
Highways between invisible cities
Caught in the undertow of the quotidian
Paycheck to paycheck

RYAN MURPHY

Radio Sun

If I could pare
and drought
the ever expanding
of winter.

To feel whole
against the
breath shattered
night sparking.

We've brokered
this peace before:
locate yourself
in the path
of abundance.

Come alarmist
cannon-fodder
tassel in your tricorner.

RYAN MURPHY

Sea Level

1.

Socket violence
bludgeon to begin.

Dry leaves rattle in a wind's
eddy perfect

October sprawls
from horizon to

horizon.
From which the hence
of anxiety broke.

I will burn all of my shirts.

You begin to prose.
Disloyal quiet as misread
when twilit

its own fortune

2.

Morning comes
in its big white hearse.

Then sudden and sour,

salt-glass and respite
(your mute mother)

and offer or regret.

Together we unspool
the cassette

with our fingers
on the bed

and sit in that shiny
black sound.

RYAN MURPHY

Await a Windfall

Try to mean differently,

and not throw up.

Sun spindles to its last

in the rusting hulk of sky,

stars sick as knives.

We are bound together

by their vague threats,

kindnesses,

teeth like sleeping dogs.

Or I pistil in heat, is summer sleep.

Bludgeon and unspool

Thunder-cloth like bad weather,

portent,

whistles up .

LISA JARNOT

The Clark of Space

Nipples first, then the
curve of youth,

not one color
more than another

not a
big dog

or a
small dog,

each elevator,
each elevator shaft,

each pair of lungs,
each job description

on the side of a snowflake,
every ounce of every anarchy,

gratefully, not listening
to the signs.

JAMES MEETZE

Paper Narcissus

Whose marble figure and laurelled crown could be electric, admired
enough to hum like the young poet or fall into an opening field.

October's endless ribbon in a maiden's hair I unravel, unknowing
of my disorder and ill reflection in this lily'd pool.

Whose wit and winsome idea to orbit, then make landfall like paper
birds do, like waterfall, like why are we all crying.

I'm lazy about writing these gossamer words, but what else is there
when October's burnt focus is on everything but me.

Whose deep noticing could force a paper-white narcissus in water
or make red paper more simple than reworking the legend.

The landscape of the human face—like my face in a mirror, returning to
places of childhood: home, destroyed home, a chimney, smoke.

Whose refugees congregate and are praying to whomever for what
they've lost: a little space, many tears, an ashen pool.

I think constantly about fashioning an ideal self that is this but with more
money and things and time to use these tools.

Rain is inside me and inside the soil, it is mud peeling off Rose Canyon below a contentious idolater, and where the earth may split.

All of these things are happening now, like your heart is beating inside you; and I, always traveling, wish it were inside me.

GABRIEL GUDDING

Live in the Sensations of the Body

    i saw yr
    stu
    pid body
    had no or
    gans

    i had
    my eyes
    u had
    eyes
    too

    the grind
    of co
    ast on Frida
    ys

    yr bodys
    pissed a
    n iceland

    passed
    its noiselet

fo
unded by
a slap

funded by
an an
us

busy
its lip
s a force
in fo
am its lips a
fact
at fo
am

then we le
ft the mo
onba
lls to(o)
the
ir fertile hi
lls

and furba
lls fell fr
om sad
dles
and lintba
lls ro
lled fr
om battles
and eyeb
alls stir
red i
n go
ggles

a
nd we put th
e pills ba
ck in the
ir back in
the
ir back in
the
ir bo
ttles pu

t the pi
lls ba
ck in t
he
ir bo
ttles

and n
ow aga
in a body
's in its or
gans in i
ts orga
nic lo
oms

GABRIEL GUDDING

Enjoying

We enjoyed Granada, we met amusing people there, there was a big park by the sea and a spattering of croquet balls abandoned in the grass, wooden planets, moreover there was a cow and a well and a thing brightly hanging on a high brown barn—we walked from picnic to picnic, a little chain of picnics out to the east, and at the last one a small man with a lone banana showing us his nickels, he kept our attention for a long time and then, like all of those days, it just kinda vanished.

DAVID HUDDLE

Need a Body Cry?

I developed a little crush on one of the robots. The object of my affection was Domo, a man-size machine with a buff torso and big blue eyes, a cross between He-Man and the Chrysler building; when it gripped my hand in its strong rubbery pincers I felt a kind of thrill.

Robin Marantz Henig's review of Love and Sex with Robots, The New York Times Book Review, *Sunday, December 2, 2007*

. . . bodies are disgusting and I prefer not to think or talk about the things that happen inside of them.

Sara Henderson

Should a body meet a body
Coming through the rye,
Should a body kiss a body,
Need a body cry?

Robert Burns, "Comin thro the Rye"

Robot Love—I'm talking Biblical,
not your garden variety Platonic—
has infiltrated our little temple,

and here you thought your basic
sexual configuration was all set—
you liked skinny men with sardonic

smiles or sad middle-aged brunettes
who insist on committing the deed
in the presence of their Siamese cats.

Available online nowadays is a machine
guaranteed to stroke your little boat
farther out to sea than you can even dream,

its heart's a box of chips, Elastigel butt
to make you blaze up into flowery fire,
a thing programmed to talk genius-level smut.

Today, on the phone taking my book order,
a woman's voice shot me that kind of thrill—
no body, no body, but oh Lordy, I wanted her

to have my babies. Addled, I began to tell
her about Robot Love, how it was up to her and me
to save chaste desire before it skedaddled all to hell.

Of course she said no. Very sweet. I could see
her clearly—Birth of Venus by Botticelli,
something from Genesis or maybe Deuteronomy.

SOMMER BROWNING

The House

is shaped like candy. And the candy inside its dribbling refrigerator is shaped like mouths. And the house. It sits on a hill. And it is shaped like a hill. It's shaping, its flat parts peak, its inside furrows then opens to grab you. Then, you are shaped. Now, you are then shaped and your then shape punctures the house. Something nuclear. Something west-end and beachy. You are still at work. Like the men.

SOMMER BROWNING

In the House

the most boisterous of breasts will quiet if alone. So hope they are never alone because us lonely is art. Their symbol will divorce us or overdose or Ambrose Bierce and we'll cardboard, ironing blouses forever, tied to chunky furniture.

SOMMER BROWNING

Beside the House

the women whose heads were shaved are on the telephone, not digitally, but like birds. Their slick heads grip the wires. All the ice in their mouths is melting. Below, thirteen machines busy themselves with origin, lacey shadows filter across their backs.

SOMMER BROWNING

In the House

the plaque next to the dishrag reads, *textile, c. 2006*. Next to the couch, *anonymous, mixed media, 1994*. A whisper whispered, the respectful crowd refuses to eat an apple on the counter. *When the phone rings, talk to Yoko Ono.* By which crafted hand strewn about these bills? *Please describe the process of your work.* A baby is born. Then she is housed.

SOMMER BROWNING

Outside the House

is an earth mover, you call it a backhoe. It is a scar, you call it cicatrix. Excessive and injurious, once you leave the house. What swirls at your ankles, sticks. All the scraps in your pocket are yours. You'll be known by the way your folded hands unfold. Before that, sun gathers in them like a mob.

EVAN KENNEDY

St. Francis's Pastoral

Being born stable before the saber rattling
began bucked my bell empty.
Though oft times dragged through
the town's bannered ghost-rot, I
clamored toward friendship's
crime-crusty shackles.
                      Thin-bearded, I rang
a brimming measure of lines and
planes in relation. Unannounced
changes striking atonal— Missions
and motels nestlin' in new latitudes—
As garland-grinning spires sewed me
into a suit of worry, birdsong recircuited
thoughts of my soul's attrition.

EVAN KENNEDY

Holiday, Celebrate

O wind winding pollened ribbons
round our founding fathers. Brave
souls, weathervanes a-tugging wafting
wonders. Stutter, scents, as someone
shepherds th'ample curves of
air. Communiqués tunnelin'
underground— In town, boys stir
in hobby. The harvest rag raised—

ARLO QUINT

Easter She's My American Monday Best Friend Music

    be sure to breathe in tomorrow
    the feel of mind being where it is
    together with what turns way out

    how the weight of unnoticed world
    rallies most of personal history to a point
    kicking through the falling leaves

    covered by a sign of what's to come
    on the long walk down to lost lake
    blue and red seconds of the close stars

    nightsky with turpentine seldom abstract
    taller folded higher exit over flower all
    hands the certain stretch of highway

    over complicated graphics of love
    rises an end in the sight drain of line
    left in the lyric dust late in the night
    left in the early other dark thought

ARLO QUINT

Now Crop Range

dreams in one motion
can smooth things over
and raise up harsh sound
to sleep for common life

one experiment is to alter
basic terms in the world
continuing against ghost
you rode in on three things

don't send mysterious circumstances
in the country where you hit your
head the sun comes up because
you don't wash your hair

there's nothing
or a divided heart
don't read any further
or go without saying

DANIEL NESTER

<— —>

from *Queries*

being a collection of questions, reservations, and comments written by the author in an attempt to absterge and clarify elements of student and postgraduate creative work, 1995 until the present time

V.

WOW! This is new, surprising, strange, out-of-nowhere, and oddly sensual. Perhaps be particular about this? Does the speaker have a particular exotic location in mind for the erotic encounter with Freddie Prinze, Jr.?

Lose these adjectives, and perhaps some others. In this case, I think we can agree that all blaring alarm clocks are "obnoxiously" blaring, so it weighs down the writing.

The play with Prince/Prinze in the enchanted forest is an inspired one, as is your choice of the name of Sam—perhaps give Sam a last name to be parallel to Freddie's? I know this is a first draft, but especially in a run-on sentence-heavy paragraph such as this, punctuation is especially important so we don't get taken out of the dream of the writing. It's worth fixing, however—this monologue is hilarious, and is a great start.

I know that you are serious here . . . when you describe this with your dog, but I think you should probably also take into account that you're doing a bit of personification here, otherwise known as anthropomorphism, even what is called The Pathetic Fallacy (sounds worse than it is). I can also take this line to be in the voice of a younger girl, and so I can believe the sentiment.

Oh I love this, and you know I want you to describe the centerfold, and perhaps even explain why Aunt Tess had *Playgirl*—was she a subscriber? A *Playgirl* fan? Was it an abberation that Tess would get a porno mag?

More detail here? You're depending on these haircuts do a lot of work for you in this line—maybe add another sentence without an I remember—it's not against the law, doncha know—and take the opportunity to give these haircuts their proper representation.

In a story as short as this, switching back between Martin and Luther can get confusing? Just a thought.

Just say "said." What he's saying—or it should be evident what he's saying—*is*, in fact, 'reflective.' So the idea is to get around writing things like "reflective." You could have him scratching his beard, looking up into the sky, something that would enrich the reflective stuff he's saying here. He is, after all, Martin Luther, and he's talking to Saint Augustine.

DANIEL NESTER

from *Queries*

being a collection of questions, reservations, and comments written by the author in an attempt to absterge and clarify elements of student and postgraduate creative work, 1995 until the present time

VI.

Oh, I see: you mean that the cat could be staring at the fish instead? I think you could probably put these two lines of dialogue from Oreo after the "tired of Josie's antics" bit. It would be a better setup, I think. Curious to see what the group thinks.

Do you mean gerbil meat? You might want to get the "sits on top of the gerbil cage" bit before the "real deal." This is so nice!

Think of it this way: Is it more important that Craig helped give birth to the goat, or that fact that he said it proudly?

Would a person named Gunter with a German accent really say "You shonuff weezing an' hollerin' now, ain't ya, mama?"

This dream your narrator has of Freddie Prinze, Jr. occasionally gets a little involved, convoluted. Are they in a bungalo in Tahiti or still in Bayonne?

Why would Blair = Freddie? Blender drinks?

I'm not sure you would want to have to tell us that it's shocking and horrifying. If the secret about the Cyborg is really shocking and horrifying, then let us decide?

I know that in our previous workshop you were resistant to addressing this, but perhaps in revision you could look and find some things to firm up and emphasize more: one theme I am drawn to here is the idea of parts of the body severed and reunited. The amputee, the rings—I guess were are talking about limbs.

Who is the "our" referring to in stanza 3, for example? Is it the "I" of the poem as well as "Unchained Freedom," or a person addressed in the poem?

Why is this dude naked? Also: Watch your participles and gerunds.

By "trance-like state," Do you mean "nodding off to sleep"? Would your child narrator know what a "trance-like state" is?

A glass explosion? The sound of glass exploding? An explosion of glass? Exploded glass? The glass exploded and jolted me awake?

Andy is a she? Change spelling to Andie, as in actress Andie McDowell (sp)?

Perhaps a missing bit of descriptive language of how Andy and Max are, at this point, intermingled. Is it one behind another person? Are they entwined?

Shape-shifting implies that Solomon could shift into different shapes, right? Seems like a static form of the condition if he is "only" a leopard.

Is there another way to characterize—or another way to lead up to it—this occupation as a "mate"? May sound retrograde or chauvinisitic to some readers, even in reference to unicorns.

Why does it matter, in the world of this story, that it's a new iPod? Interesting, I think, but it might throw us off.

Why specify this? Because he's around all this other plant life? Might not be that important.

DANIEL NESTER

from *Queries*

being a collection of questions, reservations, and comments written by the author in an attempt to absterge and clarify elements of student and postgraduate creative work, 1995 until the present time

VII.

Wouldn't it be evening if the lamplight was visible? Why not just lamplight?

How would Harold know if Andy and Kate ordered said bulldozing? It might have been some other person, yes? Or is Harold reading this sign and thinking that it's a contractor that the couple have employed?

Is it important that the soil is upturned here? Oh, you mean bulldozed? Upturned could mean anything, like the dog had dug it up, or there's been some gardening.

Why is shit—or at least the hit part—in italics?

The only way this would work is if the word dog was a collective noun, like man, in reference to them being better lovers than men. Or if you had referred to a specific daschund in the previous sentence.

I'd choose something more specific than "emanated a vibe." It didn't mean much in the 70s, and still less now. Do you mean it has some kind of otherworldly power? An aura? Try to be more specific. We're talking about a breed of dogs who seduce women, so the language should be specific.

You're going back and forth between "the porno," which refers to a specific film, and "pornography," which is a whole genre of film, an idea. I would try to choose one and use it consistently, since each connotes a different meaning for the reader. A specific film would open itself up for in-depth description of the film itself, while pornography in general could be described as something he watches as a general practice. But since you're describing one day, it strikes me that you can't use both.

The daschund's drool? Or Harold's?

How can eyes burn with hatred and still be watery?

How about just a dog? Here, your daschund is melding perhaps a little too closely with Harold's often Hamlet-like interior monologues, which I like.

What happened to the coffee and crumpet request? Does Harold, in fact, make him a cup of joe?

See my note re: pornography vs. "the porno."

Don't really know what you're saying in this sentence. Is there some prequel that talks about the others?

But it's their former bedroom, right? And, by killing the dog, which is what Harold wants the crew to do, it will soon be his again, right?

Just because something is ambient doesn't mean it can put one to sleep. I think you're thinking of ambient music, but that usage doesn't translate here.

The gerund here implies that he went to sleep (i.e., retired) and then inserted a video. Or that the inserting set for a process to begin him getting in bed. To have this make sense, you would have to have the word "and" before "inserting."

So—is it Harold's delusion this dog-effing is happening? What's the real deal? And what does the porno-watching have to do with this?

Do you mean to say they stay the entire night during these processes? Not clear, and if it is the case, it might explain why that creepy crew guy was next to the TV that night.

Wait—they have fangs now? I thought they just looked alike, but were human.

Here and elsewhere, change your sentence structure to active voice with direct syntax. Here it would be: "The little man broke out of the throng, his tight pants . . ."

Is this person also the little man?

SANDRA SIMONDS

My Lyric Sensibility is Gone

Oxygen float on.
Pilgrim to Canterbury.

It's really incredible!
I'm no longer a poet but a

Nauseating ward
Where peroxide halls frac-

ture to the sound
Of nurse shoes on lacquer.

They say genius knows
itself. What a belligerent

mess. The sound of bed
pans in a pigsty. They say the imagina-

tion should be able to con-
trol itself—hold opposite

Poles of
Magnets together

To make whole but
I'm not Greek stone.
I can't hold

Onto these storm
white sounds

where the pot
boils every part.

SANDRA SIMONDS

I Am Small

but my life is enormous.
Huge as angels.

Huge as a zookeeper's
Heart. Who knows

How large the
Zoo is when you take

Into account
The surface area of all

The cages. Not to
Forget the aorta. Let's get

hitched in the
roomy cage of

the latest newly extinct
species. He's

gone. There's room.
In this country

they make lists (in
hieroglyphics)

of all the unions
that have ever taken place

and all the unions that
will ever take place.

There's no way out of this one, Sam.

That's what they call a nation.
That's when they ask the syringe

and turkey baster
holding zookeeper

to sedate
The elephants

And artificially inseminate
The blasé Pandas.

SHANNA COMPTON

*Young America, in a Dress Coat at Seventeen,
Finds Them All to Be Monstrous Slow*

Having neither a remarkably fine figure
nor a Paris gown

nor a distinguishing talent
for piquant conversation (in public)

she nevertheless has had ample leisure
to observe her sometime suitor's

devotions to shallow,
overdaubed, underdressed women

& scorns the cheap stimulus
as chief social pleasure

develops a little sourer,
an active, intense individuality

*

Names spoken lightly in evening,
the prolonged enchained attentions of a man

—the attentions which women would not be women
if they did not like to receive—

all the goings and comings
of Summer days by the sea,

fall to the class of
frivolity & flirtation

*

Poor censure.
Perhaps she should write a pamphlet.

*

Becoming more and more extravagant
in her dress & habits

she is forced to surround her person & home
with the sensuous attractions

by which the demimonde
allures loose husbands away

She might go further,
might be less lavish in outlay
& more modest in dress

if she were led to suppose
that men liked it better

JOHN KOETHE

As I Woke Up One Morning

As I woke up one morning
In my solitary bed,
The colors of a delicious dream
Flickered a while in my head

Before fading into day
And the early morning news
Of someone waiting for a promise
Of the life that time renews,

Even as it takes away.
The day stretched out before me
Like a duty waiting to be kept,
Like something boundless and free

And yet to be completed
By what sleep left in its wake—
To come back as something beautiful,
To be loved for its own sake

And for the love it might bring.
I heard the hint of a song
As I lingered before the mirror,
Sure that before very long

It would all feel new again,
If only for a few hours,
By dint of an inconsolable
Imagination's powers

Of transcending time and space
Before falling back to earth.
Like a king who travels from afar
To be present at a birth

That in its "hard and bitter
Agony" seems more like death,
I was the sovereign of my kingdom
Of one room, where every breath

Brought me nearer to the tomb.
The paths of least resistance
Lead to dead ends. I thought I saw it
Beckoning in the distance

Like a friend just out of reach.
Why are poems and life so hard?
Is there a place where the forgotten
Things I'd labored to discard

Might still be waiting for me?
You who listens and pretends
To care about these abject musings
On which my whole life depends,

Do they mean that much to you?
Wouldn't you prefer instead
Brief entertainments to pass the time
Until the time comes for bed?

In the dream I'd had that night
—And oh, to have it again—
Something seemed to answer from the air
Like a life poised to begin,

As the words found their places
On a page, and in the gloom
The gold gathered the light against it,
And you were there my room.

CATE PEEBLES

Waiting for the Sweet Imported Fruits of Distant Shores

What have you done to me, smithereens?
What do you intend to do with those
peaches and that crate of elastically wasted

romance? There is room in the foyer for at least
one more. Alright, already—I think we
understand how to tumble into the

shrubbery & blame it on bramble. I wore a hand
tooled balustrade for weeks & allowed
renovation to commence on the flying

buttresses in my rotunda. Filter the moat!
Place me! Place me lightly on the credenza
beside the figurine of Heathclif, hunched

& looking gloomy. Sometimes it's simply easier
to be detestable & porcelain & broke, because
the clearest thought you ever had is never

enough to boast of. It comes back to me in ribbons,
how we taught ourselves dead languages
to uphold a certain level of liveliness after

carving roasted parsnips & boar, assuming
there would always be one more galleon of Oolong
headed our way. Fortune settles in a cup &

foolish me left gazing at my candied navel
orange, bright & orbiting the pole
where my soul should be—right here,

tucked under the shoulder blade.
I can show myself to bed & make nice
accordingly. Tonight, forget the story book

but not the glass, not the ice. Feelings will be
felt or felt up & taken home before
midnight in a regatta of seeded pumpkins. I look

for lanterns through cracks as I hobble down
the hall. The carpet chokes between my toes,
the banister's got an iron spike against my

ventricles & the bathroom switch won't flick—
Does this always have to be my face,
or can I exchange it for something foreign,

something squiggley & backwards, or left-
handed at least? My pulse keeps coming
up like the wives of Henry VIII upon the block:

I am scheming from the rooftop, scheming for
the arrival of my bearded twin & all his undone locks.

MIKE HAUSER

Make Forth With Pleasing Syllables

that mysterious formation of moon black eye
this prick pushing a stroller
as if we don't have knowledge of hell
many raccoons trapped in dumpsters
will be moved to daydream
violent hallway of a modern instant
plush rabbit fur laurel
changes you into gentle microwaves
the irreducible buffet of literature
communicae rents a whistlestop tour
something that might make sense now
but will see us to in the adorable
warm dispute as like undressing
in front of human lamps
everyone knowing there are no groceries
there were never any groceries
but no one's saying it

MIKE HAUSER

Only the Fawn Hall

our country's getting too soft
too overcome with wigger flaps
juxtapostion of cable with anvil
epilepsy pro with store credit
like reading a jung book is magnanimous
slash the current occupants are wide recievers
every other interference a performance
in the tabernacle mosh hyperbole
bowling veterans in the alley seem nice
then you start talking to them
like backwards silent movies
in the low visibility mist
someone named 'billy' speaks thy name
the collapsing villain at the end of the rainbow
a cross billowy big message gambling
perforant as witty spokespuppet
the zap that quickens our hearts
is only the pie in the aisle

BUCK DOWNS

post hole digger

we are what
  ambition
has made us.
and there ain't nothing wrong
   with a repeat customer

the bulk of the blues
flogs the flame
   into the lightness

   southern time zone
   simple mcsugar
leftover treasures of the season

   turning around to see
what the sound of broken
glass was all about

retrieved another
discarded plaything

& there it is
one of my alternate
lives in the sunshine.

BUCK DOWNS

⟵ ⟶

sucky leven

   I slip
in my waking
and wake to start
   it over.
knockout white
  box of gelt
at the candy.

cigar box transcriptions
hellen keller corduroy
redbush petitioner
in translucent parte

    holy caterpillar,
 I want your
 undivided
 attrition—

    zero morning star
    in a corner of the corner
    cut the cord

AARON BELZ

So This Is Tuesday

So this is Tuesday.

So this—this is Pontiac LeMans.

This must be what they call
windshield wipers.

So this is Roddy Piper.

So this is macaroni.

This is what all the fuss is about.

It's Anchorage Alaska all
over again.

So this is elbow macaroni.

So this is K. D. Lang.

And this must be her left boot.

That would make this her right boot.

So this is what it feels like
to walk down the street, alone.

So this is the famous persimmon tree.

This is what Rowdy Roddy Piper
was telling me about.

So this is the most famous tree in Canada.

This must be what they call
"Margaret Atwood's Revenge."

So this is that hit single
by Michie Mee.

So this is what they play—
the DJs who can't see.

So this is the waste land
behind that one grocery store.

So this is what all
the swaying grass is for.

So this is my time sheet.

And this—this must be a very old ghost

come to tell me where to post

my time sheet.

AARON BELZ

The "ARRGH" of NCAA Division I Women's Swimming

Today's bad news is double: Not only did I not set any records in the NCAA women's 400-yard medley relay championship, I did not even place. To make things worse, I am not only not on a qualifying swim team, I am not on any team, in any sport, at any level, nor am I a woman. Nor do I *even know how to swim*. This is, as they say, the straw that broke the camel's back. I feel that if I knew how to swim I might be able to get around the other disqualifying factors: have a sex change; respell my name; forge a birth certificate that says I was born in 1989 (to replace the diploma that says I graduated high school in that year); enroll in a state university and try out for the women's swim team. But what if that university were not Division I in women's swimming? Then I would have wasted my trek back in time and across gender—a thirty-five year old man in the body of an incredibly athletic eighteen year old woman, yet a young woman still destined to live about as average a life as a man approaching middle age might expect (or have expected, so many years ago, when he himself was eighteen). In sum, I feel now more than ever that I have missed my chance not only to win or place but even to participate in the NCAA women's 400-yard medley relay championship. Indeed, I feel it now more than ever before.

NORA ALMEIDA

Small Time Thoughts

no matter what the distance, it is always thinkable

Edmond Jabes, "Little Limits to the Limitless"

a thing can never be finished
winter every winter for 6 years we waited
for the goldfish to finally die remembering you
as a large and almost entirely benevolent character
in this way affected by projections
where traditionally the names go on
the bottom right and lastly
I left the door open
and have not the strength
spare cables and maps
I can't bring myself to
as the gravel cannot wrest itself
from the mound
things fall into our ditch when we aren't looking
or thinking about a shovel
I am still here
leaning against the garage
somewhat like the dying garden
the mean untended sleep
the hall lamp and where it starts being dark again

I love you
in dreams where you become poisoned
a whale is there as a place holder
for the far off thing I hope to start believing in
fork-lifts and the great divide
plant a tree there and when it is taller than you
the advice continues
dawn is often depicted as a line
and that rectangle stands for a building
or a disembodied elevator
other titles we considered did not ring
as we hoped they would ring
the juice breaks down
and the sugars sink to the bottom
like small bits of metal I imagine
the ground-floor and up
the door at the end of the desert
and if I could walk there
or ride upon a small moped
I would remind you that when you swallow
the small blue capsule
you will have a sponge lizard in your stomach
perhaps forever like pathological hilarity
what you meant when you spread your arms open
and said "this much" almost brought me to tears
and made me think of the ocean
as I saw it once in a painting

MICHAEL CARR

Fur Sites Revamped

get it a spewing rear window
somewhere on the screws
woody sex fights down the pecking

route, I'll call back, got a sec
or wink your guy. And you

somethin' party yeah,
not very cherry
but it's an oldie goodie well
it ain't they got

a '30 to know they're
either still up don't where I wanna go
you know I get to all you gotta

MICHAEL CARR

The Captive

your house is pretty it's
substances are in foster programs
tendrils of dense flush rising
the latent plaza's twin
death witness
her I would recognize in a crowd
sprung from the
fact some small amount
participate in my wishlist
by rutted shade hid
wary and preoccupied by mild
hunger far through the winter
into the distant provinces
a felon would whisper
obscene new technology
now that it's closer
the whiteboard is sad
becoming expert on rain
cycles and crickets
an immunity you never planned
in Mexico once
none the wiser no sushi bar
snaking through back
streets parents disappear

the animal with camera
advocacy notices
this is what I feel happens
your prayer for relief
comes seeking a temporary
injunction alighting
in small homage to
children having known
contact partial service
and neither of us show
left with the former benefits
delocalized within
the antechamber shallows
core flashed out
honest whether it's
true or not found within a vicinity
totem dimension
our exact license caught off
guard to a complete sense
of royalty american
boy style away for a minute or two
held past the park
in safeguard for night

MARK HOROSKY

Fifty Foot Trailers

Sure, sooner or later. In the months that end industrial-sized. On overturned carriages, stacked pallets, and bales of cardboard. Dislikes: human-like sculptural renderings, the dream life, innumerable tombstones. Leaving it alone as it is here: sunlight is sunlight and parking lot is parking lot. Allowances for all-nighters: nightcaps. Brown paper or Ziplock. Tired still wants to make money, ditto injured, include disturbed. Tonic accents among the tonnage. Some prefer the aluminum foil, napkin-wrap, or Tupperware. Warehouse. Monday through Friday except for most holidays. House of wheres, whens, and howsoever. Amongst the compactor and insects, smoking and not eating at all. Rabbits in the rabbit brush are worth a Rabelais. Men gain weight in their abdominal region. Men bla-bla-dee, bla, bla blame them? The clocks couldn't be more specific.

MARK HOROSKY

Harbour

It's the lateness, largely elapse, a low fidelity. This maybe the interstate or just into the mist, and in the midst of, and not just the end. "A small moment in a multitude of moments, blanks, volumes, smells, employments, and a feeling . . ." Radio in the ear in the song that's languorous and loyal to him in every verse. These evenings are a promise of cancellations, unhurriedly dark, an uncharming chiding, fondling intuitions, into which tankers drag a tide. He Buicks. He is yet another attention. Which is to say he is mostly a sympathetic spreading. While some other cars, true, then. Like the people it locks in with lovemaking and manufacture, rancor and loons, blooms and bygones, the landscape grows older. Like the pier the Atlantic tenders petulantly. Like the radio dark. Like his sneakers stitched with an emblem of flight.

MARK HOROSKY

Laundry Hints

It's easy to feel naked when your clothes are off. When your clothes are off, it is easy to feel less than the wail of a siren. Clothes for your loathes, array for your disarray, dress for your buttress. Always test on inside seam for colorfastness. The laundry is candid, the dirt of quotations, so it leads to an awful purity. We have a box, a Scotch-taped basket for laundry and the hell rest we throw in it. Glamour comes while were wondering still as blocks of wood, and, incompleting sentences, the thunder that doesn't thunder, and we choose encumbered like traffic, with our hands meaning dwell, the loner shirts alone. Sure, shine when the moment's sudden sugar sweeps, but no one wants to talk with us when we feel mouthy. Today we wrote, "Sometimes clothes feel like a criticism." Don't blame us. You won't find anyone who blames *you* here.

JESS MYNES

Austin, TX

for Farid Matuk, Scott Pierce

single yellow
        leaves
 lilt into
    sunlit wake budded
branch
    draped
shoots heave
    pausing
        paper wasp—
                wobbling on
            an upstream—

    caw-caw grackle
        cacophony
            trumps
day's lulled
chorus cloudless

    buzzards and
cranes

JESS MYNES

Bright Lights Charge

for Michael Carr

lordly suture as elaborate dance
kill shot to tease fondly deflated
surgeon the maleficent detest has since efforts
flare doves dowse in lemonade

to a coupe
ask for five cents

sum of sun we test
angle of sunshine and lasso summarization
ask to coronation par none
veritable exposition in two ways
parted altars a kin to grouper velour
erratic into do not status

the plus posits to falter proceeds
a windy road forward
vows constant falsies be

conductive limp wrist verification though flowers
chock in startling décor
that the genie atrophied shouldn't pause vengeance
endless scurvy purports humiliations
line in there drowses to assimilation

options in other words

parliament mistreated speaks to miniscule
or five day old fish sputters
earwax in any event petals to since
take to mark in lions one's cause

have at it
the going is charted

CHARLES WRIGHT

Like the New Moon, My Mother Drifts Through the Night Sky

Beyond the boundaries of light and dark,
                      my mother's gone out and not come back.
Suddenly now, in my backyard, like the slip moon she rises
And rests in my watching eye.

In my dreams she's returned just like this, over a hundred times.
She knows what I'm looking for,
Partially her,
              partially what she comes back not to tell me.

CHARLES WRIGHT

Time Is a Dark Clock, But It Still Strikes From Time to Time

Whump-di-ump-whump-whump,
                    Tweedilee tweedilee tweedilidee,
I'm as happy as can be . . .

Pretty nice, but that was then,
                when our hearts were meat on the grill.

And who was it, Etta James or Ruth Brown or LaVerne Baker?
The past is so dark, you need a flashlight to find your own shoes.
But what shoes! and always a half-inch off the floor,
                your feet like wind inside them.

KATY HENRIKSEN

Russian Dance; Tom Waits

Into the petunias, my darling circle dancing Serbo-Croats. Stomp. Stomp. Stomp. Maestro. Maestro, your babushka's hanging from the clothesline. Baltica, Baltica, Baltica. Oy. Oy. Here now, play it again.

Forgive me baby but I'll always take the long way home.

Yes, for love of seeds, the seediness, the broken glass, riverbed rocks washed by oil spills. Bring me the cold borscht at once! Bring me another Pelmini, on the rocks this time, please! You must. I just put my name up on the board. One more game one more, just one more Pelmini.

Squeezebox: a body in two parts.

KATY HENRIKSEN

Sometimes a Pony Gets Depressed; the Silver Jews

new year's eve party
rooftop gin stills
oh my that's a classy hat
emily, oh emily, that corduroy's svelte
and *sometimes a pony gets arrested*

KATY HENRIKSEN

When I Was Drinking; Hem

Heavy cicada pedal steel, rolling hymn pianos, muted strings scratch, Sally's lullaby voice, it was that summer you took my job at the bookshop. Soon for Berlin, my exit from the katy-dids, the fireflies, the redbuds, the front porch lazy eyes and you.

Mylar me, help bury the dead birds we found behind the bookshelves, bake me in the muffin tin, roll me in the grass, *you and me dying everyday.*

KATY HENRIKSEN

Nude as the News; Cat Power

    mixtape temptation
    Jackson, Jesse,
    I've got a son in me
    dime novel bike rides
    sister summer city
    a gallon of rosé
    texas toast brunch
    think delta blues and
    Pavement, Georgia
    childhood, think temptation,
    raw, flame, *he's dying to*
    meet you.

CHRIS MARTIN

Some Remarks on Song

Singing reciprocates the advent of us in the world. To sing is to create an event of Being; a becoming forth that is no mere echo, but verily a response. Being is a conversation the universe has with itself. When one engages the world by way of song, she takes up the other side of that conversation, transforming Being's soliloquy into a dialogue. To my mind, this is rooted in a harmonics of need. There is a need for the world to be acknowledged, for a response to return the world's appeal to itself through itself. As Derrida wrote: "I felt the necessity for a chorus." It is a chorus of desire and wonder, the primordial wonder of presence, of the presencing that is brought forth by sense. And this is why song is always phenomenological: it is an acknowledgment born from perception and a response borne by it. It is a resonant naming, a halo to illuminate the givenness of each moment simply by calling attention to it. It is this call, this further appeal in song that returns, as the universe's light is shown and showers back upon us, perpetuating the wonder that is becoming forth. To bear witness in this way is also to situate oneself, to find placement. When the I acknowledges the world through song, it takes place amid the plenum, its own sense separating and joining simultaneously in the way of Merleau-Ponty's reversible flesh.

When I speak of presence and the wonder of its continual reprisal in the world, I approach another term, a crucial term for the exploration of song: disclosure. Song is the expression of the disclosure of the world to the singer and then a further disclosure of the world back to itself. Song opens, concomitant to a physical openness of the body and of the mouth, as indeed the world does, opening forth "that which does" or "those which do." It is an activity that illuminates the active, an opening that rejuvenates the open. Disclosure also has the valence of secrecy, which intimately textures Being in its mysterious and indeterminate wonder. Song brings us closer to what Bataille calls "the intolerable secret of being." It is the passing of a secret into the realm of the real, the texture of the real grazing against the real itself, just as the words and notes produced by man drag and catch in his own throat to create his appeal and acknowledgment. It is given to us to sing. It is one thing, in the words of a Spinoza, which a body can verily do. The call opens toward response. It is our responsibility to sing the world back to itself. There is no truth, but there are innumerable answers, the song being one of the answers particular to humans, an act ontologically given to us to do. An act of need that returns to us from the desire of the world.

CHRIS MARTIN

from *This False Peace*

It is the first   day in October and how   I burden the apartment

with sneezes   lemons from the bodega exploding   with seed

a pagoda on fire on the edge   of the lake   my nose   still running

Once I had an earthquake   in my ears   It is the first

with sneezes   how I burden   these earthquakes with whisper-talk

as we rushing make caricatures   of air   We call them

now   once   every   a finish   that chokes what it makes   shine

I did not want the abstraction   of being   out for a walk   She lied

when she   swore she   wouldn't read the moon   any longer   no

small assailant   of mirror-light   In my ears October   talk

the edge of a hyphen   of whisper-light   *Then I is heterogeneous*

electric   with broken ghosts   the abstraction like circles

for the moon   Don't use words   Don't use words   Don't use words

Getting drunk keeps   cornering the brain   and in that we punctuated

happening   but you are the one that saved intelligence   thank

god   I never wanted Wednesday   to end   never wanted

the abstraction of being   separate   The time tolls   I sneeze

The neighbors take *Silence*   out for a walk   the streets easy

with things the air might confide   incipience a flooding that adds

imperceptibly to each   wrenching turn   the surface a glue to terrify

the surfeit or god   keeps happening   a punctuation to harbor time

a sneeze   in the flood   I want to sleep in   the sleep you

sleep as *ferociously*   *one must drive on*   *to tenderness*   Repetition

is desire   I sneeze with sun   a groping wind on my arms

half-grown   wrist-wisps   from recent surgery   my pelvis not long

closed and *in the deep*   *stiletto branches*   I'm always touching

double-jointed women   Silence insists on so much noise

Neptune is in tatters   the way   the shreds of the eye project the room

in which we are moored and if   *our false light*   *stutters neon*

neon none—this   false peace reads   witness witless white

except it is now   become not "life"   but a slow explosion

all flesh become sound become a light   sound as in   *flash*

Of course it is   color this mooring   material this naked darkness

just now   perforated by Guston's pinkening   red   a wartime

color for lovers   a humming color to slide across each

island of roughness   that my hands could not stop

traveling over   as these surfaces stub   at rough light   abut

a dire ambiguity   that my hands could not stop traveling over

haptic   awake   murmuring   *of of of*

MATT HART

The Grooviest Boater of All

To a closed ocean beach on a tortoise I roll.
Heat stays, the slowness descending in a morning vacuum.
I'm not cold at all. To the infinite ocean on a tortoise.
Rolling. Descending in a morning vacuum,
unlimited first thoughts aren't sadness, they're better
than saltines. An attention to a softness in the dryer,
into a fast-moving, rabbit-fur heat.
Full-on attention. Unlimited landfill.
Unlimited ocean in sadness, a storm cloud's depression,
a dispersion in fishes. A landfill's
attentive surveillance. I am ever descending. I am ever
with tortoise. White depression trickles with blackest
departures. Onward to darkness! beside the Chinese Exit.
It is only the beginning. A Chinese beginning.

MATT HART

Skies of America

O full-throttle
that isn't a blue one,
there is a jet lag stream, and there is
a cormorant mating a rocket; the skull
of a red bird scraping 'gainst a tree,
a white-bearded goat tied up to a Lexus.
Scratch and sniff. Blueberry window.
This hurricane loves you, her name is Dreadful.
Hocus-pocus, watermelon patch.
Out in the distance, the growling of an engine:
jet-ski metropolis, Chinese laundry,
making a mess of a fit of a rowboat's glistening fishes—
just caught (back-breakingly!) for dinner.
A little white wine, olive oil, paprika.
The major general is a plastic militia.
The major problem is a flower at dusk.
Dead-headed at dusk, then carried
away with itself by the baby, shaking
and rattling her little garbage can-can.
A dance step sure, a twisting better swirling.
Weed to the weary, O butterfly churning,
not a cloud in the sky or the Cyclops.

MATT HART

My Wife on Her Vicodin Kissing

My wife on her Vicodin kissing. I wish
I had a bike made of leaves. The meat hanging
taut in the house of our dog. I wish
I had a lightning of trees. No lucky cherries

but blossoms all around me, I sleep
in my blowfish, who's twelve stories tall.
The demands of this think-tank are naturally
terrific, the deer and the squirrels overwhelming

this Fall. Raining from clouds in the orchard
above me, a tricycle writing itself in my book.
She walks upon water drinking Sauvignon Blanc
and takes a few liberties erasing my butcher.

Who writes writes prescriptions of infinite pieces.
Who hears hears the squeak of our voice
when it calls. My wife on her bike
made of Vicodin kissing. A lightning of trees

tearing through me.

MATT HART

Sunday in America

O imitation of awe and its captions' captains,
who willingly rush onto the television-green
golf course, grain silo weeping,
wingspans bright-beating
the stars overhead. O heart-light
or heavy, the lakes and the fishes,
one-eyed monster flame-ups
and torches through the night.
Everybody standing up reading the word,
betting fist after fight on the rightness of philosophy.
Meanwhile, one young satellite falls upon another
like a cinder-block sculpture of couchgrass;
a huge crowd communicating in gibberish
traffic signals. It's the moment
of radishes. And why? because I say so, and also
it's ice through our ear bones of helium—
everybody sadder than ever
in their lives. If only I could better understand
the blossoming prescription, hymnbook
open to The Old Rugged Cross.
What are those lake weeds particularly blowing,
and where are the children so terribly
lost? We can hear them playing, but not
unseriously enough to go awry, neither to the edges

nor Halloween or Heaven. But suddenly,
it's Monday, etc. Again and again and again it's etc.—
a day like any other to marvel in America,
where one decent evergreen's shocking.
Hip replacement surgery, then back
to your station. Bouquet in your face
so terrific.

JILL ALEXANDER ESSBAUM

Her Heart Already Rubbish

Her heart already rubbish.
    Her panic already damp.
Her holes already ravished.
    Her damask already damned.

Her such and such already so and so.
    Her replacement already on order.
Her job already blown.
    Her crime already murder.

Her silver already tarnished.
    Her cyclamen already sighing.
Her virtue already vanished.
    Her death already dying.

Her dip-net already wet.
    Her phlox already rotted.
Her Gabriel already at the go-ahead.
    Her curds already clotted.

Her circuitry already suspicious.
    Her coelacanth already a fossil.
Her maybe already malicious.
    Her thumbscrew already hostile.

Her scimitar already blunted.
Her brocades already aching.
Her blouse already unbuttoned.
Her hypnogoge already awakening.

Her confession already shriven.
Her fate already in disfavor.
Her concession speech already given.
Her story already over.

JILL ALEXANDER ESSBAUM

Lust In the Time of Geometers
Or: Putting Descartes Before da' Whores

Care to let me approximate your pi to my eleventh digit?

Are Euclidean me??

ROBERT KELLY

Elegies For the Obvious

1. The Exaltation

Exalted obvious
sun in my small eyes
how much information
flies forth and back

everything we see is tomorrow
tumbling onto yesterday so fast
around and past us all we can do
is smile a word or two out
or gasp a name.

What name will you cry out?

*

It must be someone's name.
And of course, René, of course
the angels will hear you,
what else can they do?

That is an angel's business,
hearing and retelling what is heard—
do not think the messenger he is

hurries only from the gods to humankind.
An angel is all listening
and they do not pick and choose
among voices that instruct or implore them,
they hear all and tell all
and go about their business
carrying through all time and space
the name that you cried out.

2. The Quint of Fruit

The accident of morning
should be go out. Speak
before you're spoken to.
Be a bad child – there,
that is the way.

A confusion about carrots.
Or cucumbers, Praxilla.
Who is waiting, who needs to
fulfill itself in another self.
Assuming there were a self to fill.

Blood oranges in the nursery
roll. Down the back
of the nurse and bound
across the room the children laugh.
Nietzsche's philosophy is built on this.

The skin does not know enough.
The ardent suitor sighs, My will
is in my skin. The mirror cracks
to hear such accurate persiflage.
The door springs open. Cattle pass.

Along a road somewhere a man
no longer young controls his umbrella
in a patchwork wind. Sleet
or freezing wane, springlike effects
among his winter mind. Rabbits.

Upon the psaltery descanted the king's
words make a little sense, God
is on our side, after all. Uneasily
the courtiers reflect: if He be God
He must be on every side at once.
You could make a big thing of it
a thousand hands sufficed by one
controlling mind kind of big thing
but parrots would infest the moon
chilblained fingers of the latest pope.

But there are admirals, lemons, pianos,
chariots, purse-seines, steam engines,
refrigerators, don't despair. This is love
cockeyed with curiosity, never even sure
if inside is outside or the other way home.

Bananas used to come in hands
tarantulas use to come in bananas
but time is very long ago in general
time ran out long ago, time is a hat
that blew away in a warm wind, gone.

Two of them talking at roadside,
men, not close, their hands explain
the words too far away to hear. Something
that concerns them, far. One knows
how to come to it, one is not sure.

How free the candle feels without the flame!
Everything yet to come! The pale
bas mitzvah of the beeswax waits
to learn the text that will consume it.
There are other ways to think about this.

3. The Quint of Flower

Not being close enough or anything
to lick the skin of words
be with you where you conjoin
the sound of something with the glib of sense
a taste, betyourlife and elegantpain

all those fucked up botanies we try
to breed breadstuff and loosetail, rosa
lachrymose, down in Redonda
they know how to kiss, innana splits
and Sodom pies, "let me at you"

announces every monitor of sense
but the local press The Teakwood Times
is loaded with mere news, o shab
if entertainment, spillways of meant
trilobed abandoners on terrace sprawled

o you are my cabana privily
let me change in thee
becoming ready in my soul for monster sea
the pansywillow growing from my hands
to make you think of me as if I were

let come me by you in the slipstream dream
white-outs of downhill thinkers
of course it's pure comedy, its art, long winters,
Sibelius on tinny table radios, deep
woods and the sun late for breakfast

but oh the world is out of ink today
I'll have to bring my mother home
stone by stone, I'll have to think

this dreary message onto a pretty cloud
and send it skimming south to you

where you sit despising sonnets
and the portingala's blue moss soaks the wood
and dreams of Chambord's arrow turrets stir
one more pretender to one more vanished throne
Cestmoi the XVIIIth his nose stuffed up with flu

for there were few diseases when we were young
grippe and bad diagnosis and most could kill
many a child died of a bellyache
and nosebleeds carried hundreds off
while white-faced nuns sobbed by catafalques

such tiny coffins! such huge seas
to drown on Sundays! bikinis
pinned up on the arches to tell our grief,
fatal acts to trim your nails or cut your hair
or curl your tongue the way Eileen could

long before you ever heard of Darwin
except some south seas city is it
some land with stamps and kangaroos
you grow up fast around the dead
I saw them all, all dead, all night

last night marching past on the TV
Ruttmann's Berlin, spry whiskered elder
coarse enjoyers, nice dames with flower hats
all dead, all dead, maybe that little
girl playing with a rope is it is still alive

in her nineties now god knows what she's seen.

KATHLEEN WINTER

Index of Lent

a self controlled
a syllabus of errors
an infallible pope
a limit at the end of the pencil
a tender rigidity
a fragile aperture
an ill legitimate
a liquid infancy
a limpid innocence
an angel of doubt
a throes of closing
a shaped note singing
a mythical ascension
millennial persuasion
and still the stars
taken with The Very Large Array

KATHLEEN WINTER

Lament

Egg custard roses, black animal, flame
burning cinnamon, wood fire:
must these sugars make the rind,
while pulp, flesh, is this experience
of chemistry, acid and basic, too,
its bitter universal.

MORGAN LUCAS SCHULDT

Homage to Francis Bacon I

Pulverous
        the postures. Grim-

matical touchlines
co-here-ing
        as *bash*.

Big moreboys in pumps   at knot.

        Flung-fucked. Fragile.

Bald-bright
in the afterdamp.

Semi-sided—
        peenings,
    un-pent,

the bodies' rote riggings

(blood-dumb-suddenly)

       loosed. Violence

its own destined   *-ation*.

Desire-
        hack-deep; pink

&   casual.

MORGAN LUCAS SCHULDT

Song

This somewhat song.
From light to what's heft,

may I dulge it?
-*ing*uistically?

In the last of the light,
the disassembling light

(ruin-yellow blew),
may I sing them—

this duskguise,
this strew-dark,

these misflowres?
Oxygen (its sweet knees)

& in silm,
mutely.

Of this mouth
(winning soft,

occupliable)

enjoying *upclose*,
or coming

(shakesbelieve)
to *try*—its angles—

may I sing it?
From night to what's left?

MAURICE MANNING

The Simple Woman

You're right if you reckon there's something up
my sleeve this time. There is—the story

of a woman who lived and breathed and might
be breathing still for all I know.

When she got into one of her moods,
as locals termed her state, her husband

would fetch a blanket and repair
to the barn until such mood had passed.

These moods came on in the early fall,
when everything was ripe and ready;

her eyes would flicker and then she'd stare
as if she could see The Fiend himself

sashaying on a match head lit
with the empty body of a ghost.

Before I carry on with this tale,
however, I'd best make plain the word

on which this whole adventure rests.
A simple, in the olden days,

was a little weed that had a kick,
some leaves to hang around your neck

if you had a fever in your chest,
an herbal remedy for nerves;

but there were wooing potions, too,
and juice to keep a secret secret.

You could go out in the woods and pick
a basketful of simples and hatch

all kinds of subtlety. Now all
of this is chronicled somewhere,

believe me, in some old book, or locked
in the head of an old woman—now, here's

the part I've been wanting to get to—I knew
a woman other women went to

for simples, in fact, they even called her
The Simple Woman. If you wanted a man

to hurry up and woo you faster,
The Simple Woman would set you up

with seven grains of nettle pollen
and faster than a pistol shot,

that man would have you in the church
and half-way to the honeymoon.

And if the fire of love dimmed down,
you'd be surprised to see the passion

that would overcome a man, from just
the petals of an oxeye daisy—

he'd have his eye on you alright—
one dose would last him through the winter.

But woe unto another woman
who might come sniffin' round your man

with the daisy petals in his pants.
The Simple Woman didn't trifle

with anyone who'd bust-up what God,
and maybe nettle juice, had knit

together; she believed in what
was right and it isn't right for a woman

to sniff around like that, and hence,
the simple treatment was severe,

requiring intrigue and something purple—
the blossom of a burdock weed

refined into a tincture—and the gall
to visit the nosey woman under

the pretense of being sociable;
and when that hussy's back is turned

you sneak three drops in her buttermilk
and see what happens. Ole gravity

speeds up, the promontories that stood
together now commence to sag

and droop. That burdock weed could turn
a sweet potato into soup.

But our story doesn't end with that.
The Simple Woman was not averse

to plying her art for her own ends,
and once, when she was be-mooded and thus

her husband was in the barn, she spied him
in the moonlit loft. Trouble was,

she saw another shadow, too.
Now, I don't know what happened next;

there was talk, and some folks said his biscuits
tasted funny in the morning.

But I do know he stayed clear of the barn,
and for a year or so, he moped

around and just seemed puny-like
until one day he up and died,

and The Simple Woman took up her shawl
for what appeared to be her mourning.

That's about as far as I can go.
Like many stories, this one ends

uncertainly, but who knows the end
of anything, or the true beginning?

Now don't go picking daisies, folks,
or plucking burdock blooms, and stay

away from nettles—these bramble brews
and weeds are tricky. The Simple Woman,

you see, was learned in her art;
she knew what's true of every art—

simplicity is never simple,
it is obscure, and I daresay, dark.

ED SKOOG

The Boar

The glass pan breaks and the pork roast falls. Oil splatters the oven's cube. Cayenne and paprika make pain in air so we prop open the kitchen door with a broom. (Enter winter.) Snow crosses the threshold but we keep boiling the fat, peppering the neighbor. I rub olive oil under Eve's eyes while she chops more celery. Sergei opens another bottle of wine from Georgia, and from the clay bottle pours a red glacier. We swing between tasks like branches, the wine calving and the oven roaring and I think of the boar in his pen before the slaughter. That open door.

ED SKOOG

Sonics in the Garage

A cleaner pushes a surf instrumental.
A field party undertakes an investigation,
a me-like thing looking down from plane,
after many fights, asking *what?*
and music comes from that.
Bloom in May: that "artistic" feel
came back different, we recorded
and currency fell in love. Look at me
and cymbals melt. Across the bowling alley,
door broom-propped-open to smoke,
a driving beat, snarling vocal, fuzz riff,
drums and Showman amps.
Dust rides in with rainy explanations.
Fenders double-pick the orange grove
and hammer together into the canyon.
How piano on a dissected plain escapes,
I grow old farming, three-hundred feet hollow.
I'm holding you. I don't understand.
My father's study of church basements
cannot be counted on and blows dust
itself, hammer of sand, pebble, boulder,
lenses outwash gravel, strike shipwreck's
mini-fridge moonlight on clouds

My brother died in Vietnam,
nearness a bulwark for home and here,
our fundamental shore. The continent tilts
and covers the car in S&H green stamps.
The car hits the rain, bellies over stone.
Televisions are moist, temporary survivors
with audition terror. There's a guy
who installs car stereos inexpertly.
Town travel means trouble. We climb last.
Tuesday night in the practice room
unseen and maroon and zoned:
we lent them a PA and never got it back.
We must not. We're in a Thunderbird,
marking time until the Beach Boys play
the deAnza again. Where should I set
these groceries? Which hum then pop.

JOSEPH MASSEY

Drawn Out

Indoors for
days, I'm gone
in the sweep
of what
the window
gathers: sun-
set's heft serrated
between jagged
limbs hung limp
over the shed
roof's orange
rust, coils of under-
brush, the gaps
darkness articulates.

The editors of *Tight* are Whit Griffin, Andrew Hughes, and Michael Schiavo. The intern for this issue is D.R. Meriwether.

Thank you to George & Pam Griffin, Thom & Cathy Hughes, and Dominic & Susan Schiavo.

Thank you to Kevin at Mike's Place III (Deb, Todd, Ryan, Kevin, Lindy), Pangaea Lounge & Restaurant (Big Bad Bill Scully, Jay, Loni, 'Nessa), Allegro (Geoff & Anna), The Man of Kent (Jonny B. & Spoon). Kage Dawg Brouwer (stay strong), Norton Kennedy, Joyce Kennedy, Randy Frost, Big Purple, 2/3rds Skeleton, Count Sexy, Zuby, Clodagh, Hamburger Hat, Lee Johnson, Sam Clement, Dan Briggs, Chicken Dave, Missy St. Pierre, the village of North Bennington, Mile 'Round Woods, Southwestern Vermont Medical Center, Northshire Bookstore, Tanglewood Music Center, the Clark Art Museum, the Williams College Museum of Art, MassMoCa, the Virginia Toadl Davis Alumni House, Dog Ear Books, The Bookstore in Lenox, MA, Crossgates Mall, Colonie Mall, Jameson's Irish Whiskey, Basil Hayden Bourbon, and especially Buckhorn Plantation. To April Bernard, Sven Birkerts, Tom Bissell, Victoria Clausi, David Gates, Bob Gray, Mary Carol Hackett, Priscilla Hodgkins, Elaine Walters McFerron, Ed Ochester, Alice Mattison, Chris Miller, Askold Melnyczuk, Cat Parnell, Bob Shacochis, Tree Swenson, and all Bennington Writing Seminars alums past, present, and future. To the American Academy at Rome and all the 2006-2007 fellows, Aaron Belz, Anselm Berrigan, Geoff Brock, Padma, Ravi, & Emily Lundin, Brian Brodeur, Gary Clark, Susan Coes, John Coletti, Doug Crase & Frank Polach, Danté, Peter Davis, Dave King, Matt Korahais, Langston & Archie, Shirley Q. Liquor, Tom Meyer, Richard Siken, Sharan Singh, Paul Vargas, and St. Mark's Poetry Project, and, of course, to the cougars. Cougars! To Julie Agoos, Lou Asekoff, John Berryman, Rebecca Brown, Ron Carlson, Joe Ceravolo, Henri Cole, Michael Collier, Thomas Sayers Ellis, Pete Fairchild, Spencer Finch, Margaret Gibson, Lucy Grealy, Joan Joffe-Hall, Jane Hirshfield, Ronald Johnson, Anselm Kiefer, David Lehman, Marilyn Nelson, Ken Noland, Carl Phillips, Richard Pearse, Ezra Pound, Carl Sandburg, Wallace Stevens, Paul Violi, Ellen Bryant Voigt, Rosanna Warren, Afaa Michael Weaver, William Carlos Williams, Terence Winch, John Yau, and Dean Young. Thank you to Ralph Waldo Emerson. To Frank Falcinelli & Frank Castronovo (when in Carrol Gardens eat at Frankie's 457 Spuntino), Shafer Hall and everyone at the Four Faced Liar, the Blue Benn Diner, and Powers Market. When in Austin, TX eat at Guero's. When in Southbury, CT, eat at Denmo's. When in South Hadley, MA, eat at Sully's. When in Lenox, MA, eat at Prime Italian Steakhouse & Bar and The Heritage. When in Manchester Center, VT, eat at Up For Breakfast. When in Johnson, VT, eat at Edelweiss Bakery. To Senators Patrick Leahy and Bernie Sanders, Representative Peter Welch, Senator Barack Obama, Kinky Friedman, and Ethan Allen & the Green Mountain Boys. To *BookThug*, *CUE*, *First Intensity* (RIP), *Forklift, Ohio*, *Guernica*, *Guns & Ammo*, *High Times*, *Society For Mutual Autopsy*, and *Spell*. Thank you also to *Tight* (www.tightmag.com). Thank you to Michele & Justin (who found the Doctor's wallet) and to the law enforcement agencies of the states of New York and Connecticut, the commonwealth of Massachusetts, and the Republic of Vermont. To Erykah Badu, David Berman, Chuck Berry, Michael Bloomfield, The Bomb Squad, The Byrds. Chuck D, The Slowhand, George Clinton, Miles Davis, Bob Dylan, Elvis, José Feliciano, Nick Gilder, Merle Haggard, Howlin' Wolf, Humble Pie, Jimmy Jam & Terry Lewis, The James Gang, Jay-Z, R. Kelly, Alicia Keys, King Tubby, Al Kooper, Ethan Miller, Van Morrison, Thurston Moore (here's another installment fo' ya), Will Oldham, Robert Pollard, Radiohead, Keith Richards, Lee "Scratch" Perry, John "The Wolf King of L.A." Phillips, Charlie Rich, Wayne Shorter, Snoop Dogg, Joe Strummer, Sun Ra, Timbaland, Peter Tosh, Ike Turner, Otha Turner, Bunny Wailer, Steve Winwood, Witchcraft, Wu-Tang Clan, Levon Helm, Rick Danko, Richard Manuel, Garth Hudson, Robbie Robertson, Jimmy Page, Robert Plant, John Bonham, John Paul Jones, Stax/Volt Records, *The Old Grey Whistle Test*. To Geno Auriemma & the University of Connecticut Lady Huskies, The Bad Boys ('88-'89/'89-'90), Charles Barkley, Hubie Brown, Jim Calhoun & the University of Connecticut Huskies, John Calipari & the University of Memphis Tigers, Sam Cassell, Joba Chamberlain, Dock Ellis, Rip Hamilton, Allen Iverson, Dikembe Mutombo, The Big Cactus, Willie Randolph, Pete Rose, Joe Torre (Andy will miss you, Joe), Ben Wallace, the Quicken Loans Arena eateries, Shea Stadium (1964-2008), Yankee Stadium (1923-2008), and Eli Manning and the New York Football Giants. Thank you to all the small and independent presses, bookstores, record stores, and record labels that keep this shit alive and kickin'.

Thank you, eternally, to Liam Rector, Jason Shinder, and Jonathan Williams, three beloved poets, mentors, and friends whose lives and work will never be forgotten so long as we draw breath. Finally, in the words of Dr. Johnny Fever:

BOOGER!